VINTAGE HUNTING ALBUM

A Photographic Collection of Days Gone By

VINTAGE HUNTING ALBUM
A Photographic Collection of Days Gone By

First Edition November 2011
        First Printing

Library of Congress Catalog Card Number: 2011939189
ISBN Number: 978-0-940864-75-7
Published November 2011

Published by the
Boone and Crockett Club
250 Station Drive
Missoula, MT 59801

406/542-1888
406/542-0784 (fax)

www.booneandcrockettclub.com

PRINTED IN CANADA

VINTAGE HUNTING ALBUM

A Photographic Collection of Days Gone By

A BOONE AND CROCKETT CLUB PUBLICATION
MISSOULA MONTANA
2011

OFFICIAL SCORING SYSTEM FOR NORTH AMERICAN

Records of North American
Big Game and North American
Big Game Competition

BOONE AND CROCKETT CL
% Am. Museum of Natural H
Central Park West at 79th S

MULE and BLACKTAIL DE

See Other Side fo

ip to Tip Spread
reatest Spread   Spr
                      len
 Greatest Spread ei
   length, enter diff
mber of Abnormal Po
mber of Normal Patt
ngth of Main Beam
Length of First Point
Length of Second Point
ength of Third Point
ength of Fourth Point
rcumference at Smallest Place
etween Burr and First Point
rcumference at Smallest Place
tween First and Second Poi

Records of North American Big Game
183RD STREET AND SOUTHERN BOULEVARD   BRONX, NEW YORK, N. Y.
PRENTISS N. GRAY, EDITOR

OFFICIAL
SHEEP

SPECIES   Ovis Fannini

MEASUREMENTS

Length on front curve A   33 1/2"
Circumference at base B   13 "
Greatest spread D   23 1/2"
Exact locality where killed   South Fork Mountains M
                                River. Yukon Territory
Date killed   September 1909
By whom killed   Frac Fales
Owner   Annapoli   Historical Soc
Address   Anna
Remarks: This hea

a band of 20 r
moving from
162 sheep a
one half

We hereby c
on September
correct and made in a

Since the Boone and Crockett Club published its first records book in 1932, it has received an increasing number of photos from hunters with trophy entries. In the 1930s only about 15 percent or less of trophy entries were accompanied by photos, likely due to the fact that cameras were bigger, more cumbersome and difficult to operate back then. Photos for trophies taken prior to this are even scarcer. (The names, places, and animals are an incredible step back in time.) This book is as close as we can get to a time machine when it comes to visiting the past.

It is interesting to go through these old photos to see if you have ever been to the area in the photograph or if you recognize any landmarks. Several years ago, during occasional visits with a close friend of mine who is a longtime Boone and Crockett Official Measurer, I noticed he always had a magnifying glass about 4 inches in diameter lying on his desk; yet, he had perfect vision. I realized he was using it to examine the details of different firearms and trophy animals in those photographs.

Now, any chair I might plant myself in for reading has a magnifying glass for just such a purpose. (I rank highest the ones with a small built-in light.) I use it to examine the details of photos, too. What type of gear were they carrying and using? How good is the trophy they harvested? What type of rifle were they using? Is it cutting-edge design for the time period in which the photo was taken?

We don't think anything of putting a small digital camera or our iPhone in a pocket or pack when we go out today—a far cry from the effort it took to haul along all the equipment to record an image in the 1930s!

It is important to keep in mind that some of the people in these photos are the ones we need to appreciate for creating a path for us to follow, whether it be in conservation, in formulating important state and federal wildlife regulations, or simply for their role in nurturing our hunting heritage.

Let's hope that in 50 or 100 years when our children or grandchildren are viewing our photos, they will have been able to hunt, fish, and camp in the same places we did, and they appreciate the efforts made to conserve and protect our wildlife resources so that they may experience wildlife and wild places as we did.

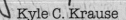

Kyle C. Krause
Publications Committee Deputy Chair

WHAT'S IN A SCORE?

You'll notice as you look through the following pages that many of the photographs do not have an official B&C score with them. When we were developing the concept for our *Vintage Hunting Album* our intent was to feature the culture of the field photograph through time and put less emphasis on the score itself. We have many fine publications that showcase trophy listings, but this one is meant to be a departure from the norm for us.

Before the scoring system that we use today was put in place in 1950, the measurements that were taken weren't calculated into a final score. The charts simply listed vital measurements for the animal along with the information about the hunter and the location the animal was harvested. You'll read many photo captions that fall into this category. In which case we only mention a spread measurement. We still have hundreds of files for these old trophies even though they don't appear in our current Records Program.

Break out your magnifying glass, find a comfortable chair and delight in the details featured in these vintage hunting photographs.

1952

This magnificent World's Record Alaska brown bear was taken on May 23, 1952 by Roy Lindsley. He was hunting near Karluk Lake on Kodiak Island, Alaska, with his .30-06 Springfield when he took this trophy, scoring 30-12/16 points

1928

Leo G. Dick traveled from Oakland, Iowa, to the Pavlof Volcano Territory near the Nelson River on the Alaska Peninsula in October 1928, to harvest this barren ground caribou (though it was labeled "Osborn Cariboo"). This caribou was later measured by the vice president of the Citizens State Bank in Oakland, Iowa, who calculated a spread of 42 inches with 19 points on the right and 17 on the left.

W.J. Closs harvested this typical whitetail deer in 1953 while hunting near the Allagash River in Maine.

1953

Record bear, scoring

1947

Currently ranked eighth in North Dakota, this typical whitetail deer, scoring 178-1/8 points was taken by Lawrence E. Vandal. This trophy was taken a half-mile south of Concrete in November 1947.

1934

1933

Official Measurer Elmer Keith was an avid hunter with at least three fine trophies in our records. He took two pronghorn in his hometown area of Pahsimeroi Valley, Idaho. The first, in September 1933, was noted to be a perfect normal head with a tip of point broken off and a 14-5/8-inch spread. The second was a year later in August and weighed 100 pounds. Its measurements were taken with steel tape the day of the kill and again January 1, 1935. It was noted that all the measurements were the same as when killed except the base of both horns had shrunk. In 1937 Keith traveled to Snug Harbor, Cooks Inlet, Alaska, to hunt Alaska brown bear. He harvested a fine specimen with the weight of the cleaned skull at 8 pounds and a length of 16-13/16 inches.

1937

1937

While hunting in Idaho County, Idaho, W.L. DuComb took this trophy bighorn sheep on October 27, 1937. This ram, measured by local hunter and official measurer Elmer Keith (pictured on the right), has an exceptional spread for bighorn sheep, measuring at 26-4/8 inches. It was published in the second edition of *Records of North American Big Game*.

1947

Earl A. Keeney took this non-typical mule deer near Sisters, Oregon, in October 1947. Keeney sent this note: "This picture shows the general lines of this set of horns. He was very old and weighed about 250 pounds (estimated). Some of the points do not show but they are there. [In] the picture is my wife.—Earl A. Keeney."

Guide Frank Tettering took Arthur E. Chandler to the Big Warm Springs area in Fremont County, Wyoming, on September 5, 1944 to harvest this Shiras' moose. This trophy bull was re-measured in 1951 by Official Measurer Colonel Gibson S. Peterson to account for the Club's new scoring system, giving it the score of 205-1/8 points.

1944

Imagine the determination it would take to travel from France to Alaska in 1906. That is what Paul Niedieck had when he arrived on Alaska's Kenai Peninsula from Cap d'Ail, France to hunt Alaska-Yukon moose. He did not leave empty handed, taking a bull with a width of 77-4/8 inches.

1906

Art Wright took this typical American elk in the fall of October 1953 on a local hunt near White River, Colorado. It was measured by Jonas Brothers of Denver and scores 378-2/8 points.

1953

Before Boone and Crockett Club instituted a standard measuring system for big game trophies, many measurements were taken at the word of the hunter. Such is the case with this photo, taken by R.H. Johnson in 1915, sent with a note: "I also enclosed a couple of snaps of an Osborn Caribou (woodland caribou) but don't remember the exact measurements; but think there were [sic] 55 points and each horn was 55 inches long. You will see by the picture, however, that it is a big head. It was shot by myself at Little Dease Lake Cassiar, Northern British Columbia, [Canada]. in September 1915."

1915

Scoring 207 points, Harvey Jurgensen's Canada moose was still the fourth-largest Canada moose on file and the largest taken from Quebec in 1947. Jurgensen harvested his bull in the fall of 1941 near Lac Gallagher, Quebec.

1941

22   It is unknown what year Warren R. Parker took this photo of the typical whitetail deer he harvested.

1946

While on a hunt at the headwaters of the Yellowstone River, Wyoming, in 1946, Texan August Jordan took this typical American elk. With a spread of 45-4/8 inches, this bull has a normal head with heavy beams and long points.

1950

Jack O'Connor took the photo of his guide, Moose Johnson, with his Dall's sheep. O'Connor harvested the ram in the Sifton Mountain Range in Canada's Yukon Territory in August 1950. This trophy was scored at 176-7/8 points and mounted by Jonas Brothers. It is now owned by the Jack O'Connor Hunting Heritage and Education Center.

This typical whitetail deer was taken by Bert E. Smith in 1972 in Spokane County, Washington. This buck is the third-largest ever recorded from Washington, scoring 179-4/8 points.

In October 1960, Bert Klineburger harvested two trophies. This bison, scoring 128-6/8 points, was taken in Northwest Territories, Canada, and was measured by Jonas Brothers in Anchorage. The other trophy was this barren ground caribou, harvested on a guided hunt near King Salmon River on the Alaska Peninsula. This bull scored 382-6/8 points.

1960

Bert Klineburger had the opportunity to be the first non-native to hunt musk ox. The permit he obtained included a clause that a scientist, Dr. Thomas J. Heldt, must accompany him and get the musk ox's brain to study. Klineburger filled his permit on February 13, 1959, on Nunivak Island, Alaska. This trophy was measured by Jonas Brothers in Anchorage Alaska and scored 106-6/8 points.

1959

In September 1927, A.W. Ruthven-Stuart was hunting in the Anvil Mountains of Canada's Yukon Territory when he took this Stone's sheep. The original measurements were taken from *Rowland Ward's Record of Big Game* with a spread of 23-6/8 inches.

1927

LEFT: In the fall of 1942, Hugh P. Evens was out scouting for elk when a huge bull crashed through their camp and scared his wife. The next day he found it and took this typical American elk with his .300 Savage. They were camping in Ochoco National Forest in Crook County, Oregon. It wasn't entered until 1994 by the hunter's grandson, Joseph S. Jessel, Jr. With a score of 418 points, it is currently the No. 1 bull for the state of Oregon.

RIGHT: Charles W. Fisher took this desert sheep during the 1972 season in Pima County, Arizona. His ram measures 182-5/8 points.

1942

1972

1968

Carlos G. Touche was accurate with his 7mm Magnum at 200 yards, harvesting this non-typical Coues' whitetail in the San Cayetano Mountains of Santa Cruz County, Arizona, in 1968. For the three years that made up the 15th Awards Period, this buck was the biggest non-typical Coues' deer, scoring 128 points.

1953

This photo was taken for a newspaper article, with the caption reading "John S. Day, owner of the Blue Moon Ranch near Medford, Oregon, is dwarfed as he kneels beside a giant Kodiak bear he killed while on hunting trip in Alaska. Day said the bear, weighing 1,400 pounds and measuring 11 feet from nose tip to tail is 'within a hair's breadth' of being the largest Kodiak ever shot." Day took this bear on May 17, 1953, on Kodiak Island, Alaska. It measures 29-6/16 points, giving it a rank of 10th for the 6th Competition.

1962

HRABAKS

On a sunny day in November 1962, Jack Grevson wa
hunting with his .280 Winchester in a local area, fiv
miles east of Stanton, Nebraska, when he took thi
non-typical whitetail deer scoring 212-2/8 points

Earl Fisher traveled from Mahomet, Illinois, to Shirley Basin, Wyoming, to harvest this pronghorn on September 5, 1951. James D. Gay (pictured) was Fisher's guide and taxidermist. Fisher's trophy meets the All-time minimum with 82 points.

PRONGHORN

1903

In September 1903, Major C.E. Radclyffe traveled from Hyde Wareham, Dorset, United Kingdom to the Birch Creek area on the Kenai Peninsula, Alaska, to hunt Alaska-Yukon moose. He was successful in taking this fine trophy. Radclyffe notes on his score chart, "This is the most symmetrical and even-shaped head in my collection, and [its] spread when killed was just under 68 inches."

1947

O.L. Steidel explains the circumstances of his hunt that yielded this black bear near Clot Creek, Quebec, Canada, on November 11, 1947. The bear was "270 pounds on the fourth day after shooting, without heart and liver. This bear was shot while I was still-hunting for deer. First shot at 50 feet at bear standing erect looking for me. Three other body shots in check at 40 feet. The bear was killed at 8 feet—jumping toward me—by last shot in head." Steidel used his .30-06 Springfield. The photo was taken in Virginia one month after it was killed. The bear is frozen solid in this photo, posed with Mrs. Steidel (background) and a friend.

1946

With his Winchester Model 70 in hand, Chas. W. Rossi trekked through the upper White River region in Canada's Yukon Territory in 1946 to harvest both a mountain caribou and a Canada moose. On August 23 he took this Canada moose, with a spread measuring a 63-2/8-inches. Two days later he took this mountain caribou, with a spread of 37 inches.

1959

Although this photo got "turned around" when printed off a 35 mm slide, it still shows Glenn P. Anderson's trophy pronghorn well. Anderson took his trophy buck near Sage Creek, Wyoming, in September 1959. Giving it a score of 82-2/8 points, it was measured and mounted by Jonas Brothers of Denver.

RIGHT: Collom McGuire was the guide for Joseph H. Shirk's Stone's sheep hunt in October 1948 and is shown in the photo posing with his trophy. This ram was taken near Prophet River, British Columbia, Canada. It was noted this was a large animal, thick horns with light coloring, and was awarded first prize at the 2nd Competition, scoring 184-6/8 points.

1934

LEFT: Joseph W. Lippincott was hunting in Chihuahua, Mexico, in October 1934 when he took this pronghorn with a spread measuring 12-5/8 inches.

RIGHT: This Alaska-Yukon moose, measuring 227-6/8 points, has a unique rack with long points that turn up and thereby prevent it from having a great spread. This bull was taken by Alex Cox near the Suslota Creek in Nabesna, Alaska, in 1957. Cox is pictured here with his guide Jim Williams.

1957

George H. Lesser took two trophy caribou in two years. In September 1949 he took the first woodland caribou near the Gander River, Newfoundland, Canada. It scores 266-7/8 points and it was noted, "His head appears outstanding because of the width of the left frontal blade and the graceful curves of the main beam." When Lesser returned to Gander River on September 22, 1951, along with his guide Olindo Gillingham (pictured), he took his second woodland caribou. This bull was significantly larger, scoring 405-4/8 points and was unique with the points on brow beams interlocked. In 1951, it was recognized with the Sagamore Hill Award. The history of this trophy is a full circle; it was willed to Lesser's son Richard, whose children named him "Woody." When Richard didn't have room for the trophy, he said he wanted the caribou to go "home" and have a proper caretaker so he contacted Harold Pelly, the stepson of Olindo Gillingham, the guide on the hunt with Lesser. Harold has the trophy and still lives in Newfoundland.

1949

G. H. Lesser
Newfoundland
Caribou
1949

Newfoundland 1951

1949

Although the title was short-lived (less than two years), this typical whitetail deer held the World's Record in 1949 with a score of 185-1/8 points. This trophy was taken by Henderson Coquat on the Apache Ranch in Webb County, Texas, in December 1949.

1907

This desert sheep was taken by Henry Sampson, Jr., on November 14, 1907. Henry and his hunting partner E. Hubert Litchfield were hunting in the Sierra Tenaga Range in Baja California, Mexico, when he took this ram, with a spread measuring 20-2/8 inches. It was noted that it was measured by Litchfield and Sampson with steel tape the day it was killed. At the time, a 60-day drying period was not required.

1932

This Alaska brown bear was taken by L.A. Cornelius near the south arm of Uganik Bay, Kodiak, Alaska, in May 1932.
The bear measured 8 feet from tip of nose to tip of tail with a skull length of 17-5/16 inches.

1949

Al Prouty
107 Second St.
Montgomery,
Pa.

In December 1949 Al Prouty took this non-typical whitetail deer, scoring 213-6/8 points, in Lycoming County, Pennsylvania. He gave this fine trophy to the Pennsylvania State Museum in Harrisburg. This buck is still ranked second in the state.

1947

In October 1947 a mule deer hunt in Okanogan County, Washington, yielded this buck with a 26 5/8-inch spread for Ben Ellwanger, Sr.

1945

On September 1, 1945, Chas. A. Rucker took this Rocky Mountain goat in the Chugach Mountains east of Anchorage, Alaska. Rucker noted, "The goat was very large and very old. He has no teeth but was very fat."

The horns of J.C. McGregor's pronghorn shrunk from the base about 3/4 inch in one year after he boiled them to prepare his trophy for his bone collection. When it was field measured in September 1935 in Flagstaff, Arizona, it was 16-2/8 inches for length of outside curve. When the measurement was recorded for the score chart, it was 15-4/8 inches.

1935

1957

In 1957, A.D. Stenger and his guide, Bob Snow (left) went 250 miles south of the Rio Grande River near Tamaulipas, Mexico, looking for jaguar. On March 9, this 16-1/16 point jaguar fell to Stenger's .35 Magnum pistol.

1966

Kelly Joachim (right) led Kenneth A. Evans (left) through Hinton, Alberta, Canada, to the north side of Grande Cache Lake where he took this typical American elk. He took this trophy during the fall season of 1966, and it scores 385-1/8 points.

Traveling from Wisconsin to Park County, Wyoming, John A. Mahoney, Jr., harvested this Shiras' moose in October 1957. This bull has a symmetrical rack with single brow points, scoring 168-6/8 points.

1957

Nicholas Biddle traveled from Jenkintown, Pennsylvania, to hunt on Charles J. Belden's Ranch in Pitchfork, Wyoming, in 1936. His efforts paid off when he took this pronghorn with a spread of 13-4/8 inches.

1958

1936

LEFT: Tom Bolack took his beautiful polar bear in 1958 on a hunting trip near Point Hope, Alaska. With a score of 28-12/16 points, it held the title of World's Record until 1963 and won 1st place in the 9th Competition. It is currently still ranked third in the state.

RIGHT: This woodland caribou with a 25-inch spread was harvested by R.D. Bird on October 6, 1936, in Point du Bois, Manitoba, Canada.

1934

Howard M. Newton made the most of his time in Alaska hunting near Rainy Pass in the Ptarmigan Valley. In 1934 he harvested a Dall's sheep with a spread of 25-4/8 inches. Two weeks later, on September 11 and 12, he took two barren ground caribou, the larger with a spread of 46-4/8 inches and the other measuring 38 inches.

1934

Glen Neigenfind, at 13 years old, took this fine cougar scoring 14-7/16 points while hunting with his dad, G.W. Neigenfind They were hunting in Sedalia County, Colorado in 1955.

1955

COUGAR

1947

The third-largest non-typical whitetail in Wyoming is currently owned by Loren T. Mahoney, but it was taken in November 1947 by his father, John S. Mahoney. He was hunting with his .25-35 rifle on a local hunt near Blacktail Creek in Crook County, Wyoming, when he took his buck, scoring 224-1/8 points.

1953

Ronnie Vaughn from Ojala Resort took Warren C. Johnston on a successful bowhunting trip on January 26, 1953. Johnson harvested a records-book cougar on Pine Mountain in Ventura County, California. It was measured at 15-3/16 points making it the No. 1-ranked cougar in California.

COUGAR

1933

In September 1933, while on a hunt guided by the Kodiak Guides Association, Reverend J.A. Wilemski harvested this barren ground caribou. His guide measured the spread at 42 inches. The reverend was hunting near Post River, Alaska, near the south end of the Kuskokwim River.

1930

Charles B. Ralston traveled from Staunton, Virginia, to an area northeast of Hunters Point, Quebec, Canada, in September 1930 to be rewarded with a successful Canada moose hunt, yielding a bull with a spread of 59-5/8 inches and a noted bell of 14-4/8 inches.

Current Member, Robert M. Lee (not pictured) did not return home to Long Island, New York, empty-handed after hunting near Gander, Newfoundland, Canada. Although it was a tough trip, "[we] walked over 100 miles before I saw a four-legged animal. This stag and two does were the first animals I saw." Lee took this woodland caribou on September 21, 1951, and this photo of the trophy, with guides Jim John (right) and Ron Francis (left) was taken about five minutes after the shot. Lee's bull scored 350-1/8 points and won 2nd Place during the 4th Competition.

1951

Enrique C. Cicero and his trusted .30-06 Springfield took two Coues' whitetail in two years. In 1966, after 10 days of hunting he took a typical Coues' whitetail near Desierto de Altar, Sonora, Mexico. This buck was taken at 150 yards and was later measured at 110 points. Cicero's non-typical Coues' whitetail took a little longer to find, but after 15 days of hunting, on November 17, 1967, he took this buck, scoring 125-3/8 points, near Caborca, Sonora, Mexico.

1967

1952

Regular Member and Record
Committee Chair, Elmer N
Rusten, from Minneapoli
Minnesota, followed his guide
Frank Bruner throug
district No. 3, in Susitn
Alaska to harvest th
barren ground caribo
on September 5, 195.
It scored 425 point
with notations of th
extremely lon
palmated point

Dr E. M. Rosten

During the 1971 season, 15 miles southwest of Endeavour, Saskatchewan, Terry L. Halgrimson took this typical whitetail deer. This fine trophy buck scores 177-5/8 points.

1971

JAN 72

Currently ranked 14th in Wyoming, William Underwood harvested this bighorn sheep in the Dinwoody area, south of Dubois in September 1959. His trophy ram scores 184-2/8 points.

1959

North Kaibab Forest, Arizona, is a popular hunting location, and in 1953 it produced this non-typical mule deer, harvested by Dale Slocum. His buck surpasses the minimum score of 215 with a score of 226-4/8 points

1953

The notable Jonas Brothers of Seattle mounted this Alaska-Yukon moose taken by First Nations Little Dave Moses (pictured below) in 1950. He took this bull while hunting near the mouths of the Hass and Stewart Rivers, in the Yukon Territory. The trophy is owned by the Yukon Historical Society and scored 239-6/8 points. It was also noted the moose has distinct waves on the face of both palms and an abnormal point on the left palm. Them Kjar, Director of the Game and Publicity department, posed with the trophy in front of his truck.

1950

1947

Avid sportswoman, Mrs. Arvid F. Benson, harvested this typical American elk in 1947 while hunting near Jackson Hole, Wyoming. Her bull scores 344-5/8 points.

Traveling west across the country from New Hampshire to Idaho in September 1960, Charles E. Dietzel harvested this bighorn sheep. He was guided by Dan O'Connor through the Lewis Creek drainage when he spotted this ram, scoring 179-4/8 points.

1960

James W. Brooks was a local to the area when he hunted the White Mountains of Alaska, in August 1955 and took this Dall's sheep, scoring 162-1/8 points.

1955

1958

This typical American elk was harvested by Mike Miles during the fall season in 1958, while hunting near Helena, Montana. This bull has extremely heavy beams and scored 384 points. Although there was a bit of a discrepancy between the number of qualifying points each side had—six on the right and seven on the left or seven on the right and eight on the left—it was verified to be six on the right and seven on the left.

On May 20, 1952, Jack Honhart took this Alaska brown bear off a slope five miles up Uganik River from Uganik Bay, Alaska. It scored 28-14/16 points.

...w.
he skull from
this fellow, the
entering for next coni-
petitios. Dawned time
May 20, 52 up
Uganik River,
Kodiak Island.

Samuel.
May your hunting days
be many.
Jack Honhart

Merle Hooshagen had two successful years of cougar hunting in Okanogan County, Washington. In January 1956 Hooshagen took the smaller of the two cougars, scoring 15-4/16 points. The next year, the cougar he harvested received a 1st Place Award in the 9th Competition, with a score of 15-6/16. Both cats were originally measured by Jonas Brothers of Seattle and later measured by Grancel Fitz.

1956

1957

COUGAR

This ram, scoring 187-6/8 points, was taken by both Lloyd McNary and J. Langer (pictured) in 1956 while on a bighorn sheep hunt in Chase, British Columbia.

1956

This mountain caribou, scoring 395-1/8 points, was harvested by V.B. Seigel on September 25, 1961, while hunting near Prophet River, British Columbia, Canada.

1961

1956

In the fall of 1956 Karl Weber traveled from Zurich, Switzerland, to Alberta Canada. Guided by Dave Joachim (pictured with horse) while near Narraway River, Weber took this Canada moose. Weber is photographed on the left with his trophy bull, scoring 214-6/8 points, which won a 1st Place Award for the 8th Competition and is still ranked ninth in Alberta.

After taking trophy mule deer in the same area in 1952 and 1953, 1954 was the year Donald G. Heidtman took the biggest one, scoring 195-1/8 points. Heidtman's mule deer hunting locale was in the Jarbidge Mountains near Elko, Nevada.

1954

1956

LEFT: Grace C. Elliott harvested this typical whitetail deer, scoring 153 points, in Valley County, Montana, in 1956.

RIGHT: This Roosevelt's elk has a 1-6/8 inch abnormal point off the top of the main beam near the right G-1 base, and measures 333-3/8 points. The bull was taken three miles south of Astoria in Clatsop County, Oregon, in November 1960 by Charles L. Smith. This trophy wasn't entered into the Boone and Crockett Club until his son, Daniel L. Smith, submitted it in 1996.

1960

In 2003, after W.E. Canterbury passed away, Jerry L. Canterbury entered his trophy typical mule deer. W.E. Canterbury was hunting with his .30-40 Winchester in the West Creek area near Howard, Colorado, in October 1951 when he took this buck. It is noted there are no G1s, so the measurer recorded the H1 and H2 measurements at the same location to reach a score of 200 points.

1951

1907

The exact location where this bull was taken is unknown, but we do know that in November 1907, Major F. T. Colby, from Hamilton, Massachusetts, harvested this Alaska-Yukon moose. It had a spread of 63 inches and was noted, as you can see in the photo, that the left antler was deformed.

1952

A.H. Henkel was hunting near his hometown of Rawlins, Wyoming, on September 15, 1952, when he took this non-typical mule deer scoring 253-3/8 points.

...hat Nora Dunsmoot started, her grandson John ...ll finished in 1996, entering his grandfather, ...ver W. Dunsmoot's Roosevelt's elk in the Boone ...d Crockett Club Records Program. Dunsmoot's ...k was taken in 1938 while hunting seven miles ...rtheast of Saddle Mountain near Coon Creek ... Clatsop County, Oregon. With a final score of ...3-1/8 points, the official measurer noted only ...5/8 deductions total—"to my knowledge, the ...st I have ever encountered on an elk."

OREGON · 1938
300·504

1938

1954

In the winter of 1954 Duane Graber took this typical whitetail deer on a local hunt in Tabor County, South Dakota. It is still ranked third for the state, and with a score of 189-5/8 points, it took a 1st Place Award at the 7th Competition.

1949

W.K. White harvested this unusual mountain caribou in 1949 near Cold Fish Lake, British Columbia, Canada, while hunting with Tommy Walker as the outfitter (pictured). Along with a score of 358-5/8 points the score chart noted, "Head does not conform to chart, measured F4, F5 and H4 taken to conform as near as possible to chart."

1956

During a special season hunt in the fall of 1956, Gene Tinker harvested this typical Columbia blacktail near Pleasant Hill in Lane County, Oregon. Measured at 139-4/8 points, this buck was given a 5th Place Award for the 8th Competition.

1956

Gloria Zerega, from Abilene, Texas, was guided by local Morris Talifson around Olga Bay on Kodiak Island, Alaska. On September 1956 she took this Alaska brown bear, which scores 28-8/16 points.

Alfred C. Pieper was hunting with his 12-gauge shotgun when he took this non-typical whitetail deer from 20 yards. This was in the fall of 1977 while he was hunting in Houston County, Minnesota. His trophy buck scores 212-6/8 points.

Although Ben Tinker harvested this desert sheep on November 7, 1919, in the northwest area of Sonora, Mexico, it wasn't measured until 1931 at the Arizona State Museum. One of the measurements, its greatest spread, reached 20-4/8 inches.

Grancel Fitz was pivotal in helping develop the scoring system the Boone and Crockett Club uses today, although he was never a member of the Club. Along with his wife Betty, Fitz was an avid hunter, especially sheep, popularizing the idea of the "Grand Slam." He also became the first man to harvest all 25 classes of North American big game that could be legally taken. Although there are few details, there are many photos of Fitz in the field with his trophies.

Follows are excerpts writing by Grancel Fitz in his book *North American Head Hunting*.

This Stone's sheep was taken in British Columbia in 1946.

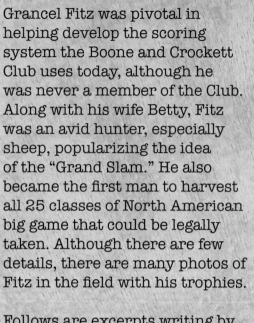

"The Stone sheep, compared to our more accessible game species, is a social climber and a Johnny-come-lately, so it isn't too surprising that many sportsmen know very little about him. The Desert sheep of our arid southwestern mountains was reported by the Spanish invaders before the middle of the sixteenth century, and the bighorn, largest of American species, made his bow in 1800. But is was not until 1897 that Andrew J. Stone brought out, from the far north of British Columbia, three rams entirely new to science."

Fitz, along with his wife Betty, was hunting in the Yukon Territory in 1946 when he took this Dall's sheep. This ram completed his Grand Slam.

Typical American elk, Blind Basin, Wyoming, 1930

"My first impression was that he looked massive, sleek, and uncommonly proud and alert. With a the rich chestnut brown of his maned neck in sharp contrast to the pale tawny gray of his body he was something to see, and his antlers showed the full twelve points of the mature bull. I'd had little experience with elk, but I know that heads with more than six points on each antler are so rare that a hunter can seldom expect to find one."

"We were almost beside a stranded log, so big that its top surface was shoulder-high. I took a couple of swift steps, rested my forehand on the trunk, and looked at the bear through my rifle 'scope. He didn't know that we existed. As he wasn't much farther than 200 yards when we first saw him, the range was hardly extreme. But he was rapidly making it longer as he traveled straight away from us, just inside the heavy driftwood along the river. He walked with that head-swinging, shoulder-rolling stride so characteristic of big bears. It is a gait that may seem clumsy. Actually, it is silky smooth in its own peculiar way."

"It always seems to shock people with no knowledge of big game when they learn that the head of a good mountain ram is rated, by a majority of experienced sportsmen, as the top hunting trophy of the whole continent. In this exalted spot our four different types of sheep are usually ranked together. But if they really deserve this honor, which I'm inclined to doubt, it seems to me that the desert ram should be rated away out in front. With equal breaks in hunting luck, and when only fine trophy specimens are considered, he is the rarest and hardest to get."

Desert sheep, Cubabi Peak, Sonora Mexico 1935

Betty Fitz with a cougar in Utah.

"This was the first wild lion that Betty had ever seen. I wanted her to shoot it, of course, but I wanted to photograph it first, and that soon turned out to be something of a chore. The tree was bushy. A maze of twigs stuck out toward the lens. After each picture, while Betty waited anxiously for the word to shoot, I moved closer in an attempt to get a less obstructed view. The lion didn't like that. It objected so much that after a minute or so it jumped out, charged through the dogs, and almost flew down the narrow canyon. I noted it didn't really run. It streaked away in great bounds, and I have a sharp-etched memory of one glimpse when, in mid-air, its forepaws were stretched far forward while its hind legs trailed straight back under the long, high carried tail."

"My first big game experiences had been with whitetails, and in the mountains of my native Pennsylvania I had learned - or so I thought - quite a lot about them. They were too easy to be interesting. A fine rack of antlers would be nice to have, of course, but after all it would only be a common deer. Now, if a fellow had a good bighorn ram, or a moose, or an elk, he'd have a trophy that amounted to something. Even a mule deer would be bigger and better."

"Hunting has given me the chance to study some of Nature's eternal truths at first hand. There were hundreds of animals that I had no desire to shoot, as they were not of trophy size, and I found that every species has its own vividly distinct personality. Meeting them in their home surroundings has been one of the greatest privileges of my life."

1961

When she was only 12 years old, Lavonne M. Bucey-Bredehoeft took this non-typical mule deer with her .30-06 Springfield. She was hunting in Weston County, Wyoming, in October 1961 when she took this buck, which weighed 357 pounds when field dressed. When it was measured, scoring 269 points, it was noted the G1 on the left antler tip was broken off. After submitting her trophy 41 years later in 2002, she won Second Place Award in the 25th Awards Program.

Charles T. Church headed north from New York, New York, in September 1924 up to Club-Triton, Quebec, Canada. The Canada moose he harvested on that trip was finally measured in 1936, with a spread of 60 inches. It was also noted to have 12 points on the right side and 14 points on left.

While on a trip to the Morley Lake District in the Canadian Yukon, Saul Blickman was successful twice, harvesting a grizzly bear and a Canada moose. The first harvest, on September 11, 1940, was the moose—evidently an old bull that was lacking points in the upper palm. Fifteen days later, he took an 800-pound grizzly with unusually dark coloring.

1940

Bert George harvested this non-typical mule deer on October 27, 1949, in the Kaibab Forest in Arizona. This buck scored 240-5/8 points.

1949

During the 1961 season, George W. Parker harvested this bighorn sheep, scoring 187-6/8 points, while hunting near appropriately named Ram River in Alberta, Canada.

1961

The history of this buck is unfortunate, as it was investigated and found to be taken illegally, confiscated, and handed over the Ohio Department of Natural resources. Eli Hochstetler originally entered it in 1975. This non-typical whitetail deer, measured at 256-5/8 points, is the fourth-largest in Ohio and is still listed as a picked-up in the book.

1975

1933

C.C. Barham and his hunting partner G.A. Adams (pictured at left) trekked over Two Ocean Pass in Teton County, Wyoming, when they took this Shiras' moose. The bull has a spread of 41-4/8 inches.

1970

Using his 7mm Weatherby Magnum, Lewis W. Lindemer took this Dall's sheep at 250 yards. He was hunting near the south fork of the Twitya River, Northwest Territories, Canada, in September 1970. His fine ram measures 173-7/8 points.

1954

Floyd A. Blick was on a guided hunt near Platinum Creek in the Nabesna area of Alaska on August 20, 1954, when he harvested this barren ground caribou. It was noted that this caribou had an unusual brow palm on the right side. This bull received a 1st Place Award for 7th Competition and is currently ranked sixth in Alaska with a score of 459-6/8 points.

Mrs. Juanita Somavia from Hollister, California, took this trophy mountain caribou, scoring 413-3/8 points while in Atlin, British Columbia, in October 1955.

1955

This Alaska-Yukon moose was taken by G.W. Berry on August 21, 1960, in the Wrangell Mountains of Alaska. It was measured by George Lesser at 228-4/8 points.

1956

KILLED OCT. 5TH 1956 BY G

LEFT: Familiar with the area, G.C.F. Dalziel worked as a charter air service pilot from Canada's Watson Lake, Yukon Territory, to British Columbia. He was hunting 15 miles east of Dease Lake, British Columbia when he took this grizzly bear. It was October 1956 and Dalziel noted nothing abnormal about the bear, just that it was big, about 1,000 pounds, 10 feet wide and 9 feet long (hanging). It measures 24-4/16 points.

1929

ABOVE: A short distance south of Banff National Park, about 20 miles northeast of Athelmer, British Columbia, Canada, R.E. Carpenter took his bighorn sheep on October 10, 1929. The trophy, at the time of entry, was located at Carpenter Garage in Newport, Washington, and had a spread of 20-5/8 inches. The marks on the photo indicate: 1) C.W. La Fors, Carpenter's hunting partner, 2) guide, required by law, and X) sheep killed by R.E. Carpenter, who took the picture.

1961

After receiving a score of 186-2/8 points, this desert sheep took 2nd Place for the 10th Competition and 10th for the state of Arizona. This record ram was harvested in 1961 by Ralph Grossman in Maricopa County, near Gila Bend, Arizona.

1914

Little is known about the pronghorn that S. Prescott Fay harvested, but included with his 1958 trophy submission was this photo, taken in 1914 by S. Prescott. The rack is that of a Canada moose and the note on back of photo reads, "one of a pair of shed moose horns found by S. Prescott Fay near the head of the Murray river, British Columbia, October 1914; at present (1958) in my possession. —S. Prescott."

With no noted abnormalities, this "very typical" Shiras' moose, scoring 158-5/8 points, was taken by John J. Huseas on September 11, 1953. Huseas was hunting 20 miles west of Turpin Meadows, Wyoming, when he took this trophy bull.

1953

1929

Stephen J. Bosworth submitted his grandfather Wallace Bosworth's typical mule deer to Boone and Crockett Club in 2009. Wallace Bosworth took his trophy with a .30-30 in 1929 while hunting in the Black Fox Mountains in Siskiyou County, California. This trophy buck scored 200-2/8 points.

1953

In 1953, B.N. Lively took this bighorn sheep during a guided hunt near Dubois, Wyoming. With a score of 185-1/8 points it is still ranked 11th in the state.

D.B. Sanford acquired this non-typical mule deer from taxidermist Jeff Seivers and entered it into the Boone and Crockett Club The buck was originally harvested by Dean Naylor in October of 1948 while hunting in the north Kaibab Forest in Arizona. With a score of 270-3/8 points, it received a First Award for the 6th Competition and still ranks ninth in the state.

While hunting in Lake County, Montana, in 1971, Darrell Brist took this typical whitetail deer with his .238 Winchester Mag. at 120 yards. Brist's buck surpasses the All-time minimum score of 170 with a final score of 173-1/8 points.

From what looks like a very prosperous elk hunt, Norman Williams' Roosevelt's elk, pictured in the middle, stands out with a score of 376-1/8 points. Williams was hunting with his 8mm Mauser in Wahkiakum County, Washington, in November 1948 when he took his trophy. This bull has exceptional G3 points on both sides, a 1-6/8 inch abnormal on the right G1 that is a point by description at 1 inch in length and 7/8 inch wide.

1948

Although Lorraine Steffensen didn't submit her trophy non-typical whitetail deer to the Boone and Crockett Club until June 2009, she had harvested it with her .30-30 Winchester back in 1967. She was hunting northeast of Hetland in Kingsbury County, South Dakota, when she took her buck. Once it had been submitted, it was measured at 185-6/8 points.

1967

1956

Even though this typical whitetail deer, pictured to the right, has a first point missing and a broken right beam, it still makes book with a score of 170-1/8 points. Harlan Francis was hunting near Blue Earth River in Fairbault County, Minnesota, in November 1956, when both he and his hunting partner successfully took these bucks.

1965

Earl H. Harris and his hunting partner from California took a trip in 1965 over to the Blue River in Arizona near the New Mexico border. Harris and his partner both successfully harvested typical Coues' whitetail. His trophy scored 116-3/8 points. Photo from left to right: "Shorty," their guide; J. McPharlin, hunter and partner; Clell Lee, guide and outfitter; Earl H. Harris with his trophy.

September 12, 1928, was a good day for Colonel Eric Fisher Wood. While hunting the lower Funny River Valley on Alaska's Kenai Peninsula, he harvested this fine Alaska-Yukon moose with a spread of 63 inches. The recorded measurements were made three years after shooting, and it was noted the spread was slightly over 64 inches when the horns were fresh. The moose also had six very heavy, elk-like brow tines (three on each side).

1928

This Canada moose was finally measured and scored in 1937. It was taken in by G.A. Blomstrom near Mine Centre, Ontario, Canada, in 1928. With a spread of 56-5/8 inches, the bull is listed in the 2nd edition of the *Records of North American Big Game*.

1944

Reinhold W.H. Eben-Ebenau lived at Slave Lake, Alberta, and claimed to have known this bear had been in the area for 10 years before he harvested it in 1944. It scores 25-6/16 points and had an 8-inch track. Not only does Eben-Ebenau own this eighth-ranked Alberta bear, he also took the No. 1-ranked grizzly bear in Alberta in 1953.

Six miles north of Dead Man's Bay on Kodiak Island, Alaska, in May 1957, Harold J. Ahrendt, led by his guide Hal Waigh (pictured), harvested this Alaska brown bear scoring 28-11/16 points.

1957

Measured while still in velvet at 352-1/8 points, Oshin Agathon's barren ground caribou comes in below current minimum score. Nevertheless this fine trophy was harvested on August 11, 1953, near Indian House Lake, Labrador, Canada.

To the Boone & Crockett Club
sincerely
Bob Reeve

Honorary Life Member, Robert C. Reeves
had the good fortune to harvest this record
Alaska brown bear from Cold Bay, Alaska
Peninsula, Alaska, on May 26, 1948. Reeves
was given the Sagamore Hill Award in 1948
for this bear, which held the World's Record
with a score of 29-13/16 points until 1952.
This trophy is currently owned by American
Museum of Natural History in New York.

Alaska Peninsula Brown Bear killed, Cold Bay, Alaska. May 26, 1948
Skull length green, 19½ inches dry 19 1/16 in + Hide, laying on ground 12 ft 4 in
" 11 11/16 " " " 11½ in. 10 ft. 4 in long

1948

Submitted in December 2009 with a score of 189-4/8 points, the details were still easily recalled about this non-typical whitetail hunt from more than a half-century previous. Earl Hodson harvested this buck in November 1958 from 100 yards with his 12-gauge shotgun while hunting Clay County, Minnesota.

1958

1964

1950

LEFT: Harold F. Mailman took this typical American elk near Elbow River, Alberta, in September 1964. This unusual rack was recorded as bordering on abnormal. It has very heavy beams the first 12 inches and the fifth point on the right antler was entered as abnormal. Given that, it still scored 382-4/8 points in the typical category.

RIGHT: Herb W. Klein harvested this Dall's sheep in the Sifton Mountain Range in the Yukon Territory, Canada, on August 9, 1950. Pictured with his native guide Paddy Jim, his ram scores 174-6/8 points and it was recorded "that the left horn was burred approximately 4 inches and the right horn curves in closer to skull and jaw by 1.5 inches."

1963

NET TYPICAL SCORE 192 3/8

NET NON-TYPICAL SCORE 303

FAR LEFT: Joseph A. Garcia and his wife were both successful on their hunt on Mundy Ranch in Chama, New Mexico, in October 1963. Garcia's non-typical mule deer scored 306-2/8 points and is ranked No. 1 in the state.

LEFT: In the fall of 1960, Berry Brooks from Memphis, Tennessee, went on a guided hunt near Burnt Timber Creek, Alberta, Canada, when he harvested this bighorn sheep, scoring 190-2/8 points.

1960

On September 23, 1939, J.C. Lenz harvested this grizzly bear on Mt. MacKenzie in British Columbia. Lenz made a note on the photo that the skull was missing, so measurements were made of the "form" used in mounting the head. Using the form to take the measurements would not qualify to be entered as an official score.

Tip to Tip Spread measured between tips of horns.

Greatest Spread

1951

Bradford O'Connor followed in his father, Jack O'Connor's footsteps when he harvested this trophy mountain caribou on September 12, 1951. O'Connor and his guide Harry Johnson (pictured, left) were hunting about 20 miles from Atlin, British Columbia, Canada. It received 2nd Place at the 5th Competition, scoring 401-3/8 points.

Duane Holt was hunting with friends Lynn Cool (left) and Ed Hunt (right) in the Sauceda Mountains of Arizona in 1960 when he harvested this desert sheep scoring 161 points.

Pat Roth posed for this photo taken for *Hungry Horse News*, Columbia Falls, Montana, after harvesting this typical American elk near Doris Creek, in Flathead County, Montana, in the winter of 1966. His bull scored 375-7/8 points.

1966

1950

Guides Watson Smarch and Johnny Johns from Whitehorse, Yukon Territory, Canada, took Arthur C. Popham, Jr. (later a regular member of the Club) hunting near Alligator Lake, Yukon Territory, in 1950 to harvest this Alaska-Yukon moose. It was measured by Samuel B. Webb, former chair of the committee that established the official scoring system in 1951. The bull scored 224-2/8 points.

Bowhunting in Wayne County, Ohio, in 1975 was very productive for Gary E. Landry. He took this typical whitetail deer, scoring 182-7/8 points, with a 45-yard shot from his 65-pound bow.

1975

1954

Texan Dan Auld took this Dall's sheep "that had no broom whatsoever, and an almost perfect head," with a score of 165-3/8 points. He was hunting in September 1954 near Hart River, in the northern part of Yukon Territory, Canada.

William F. Cruff was hunting near Valley City, North Dakota, in 1955 when he took this non-typical whitetail deer scoring 204-3/8 points.

Retired Colonel Welcome P. Waltz from San Francisco, California, traveled to Alaska for a bear hunt. On May 28, 1953, Waltz was successful in harvesting an Alaska brown bear from Right Hand Valley, 25 miles east of Cold Bay on the Alaska Peninsula. It was measured by Guy Jonas from Jonas Brothers in Seattle and scores 29-8/16 points.

1958

Fred Mercer took the No. 1 typical American elk in Montana in October 1958 while hunting in Madison County. This state record scores 419-4/8 points and was recognized with the Sagamore Hill Award in 1959. It is now owned by the Rocky Mountain Elk Foundation.

1951

Thelma Martens' record non-typical whitetail deer won a 3rd Place Award for the 5th Competition with a score of 198-4/8 and is still ranked 18th in Wyoming. She took her buck on October 17, 1951, near Cow Creek in Wyoming's Bear Lodge Mountains.

1934

Even though P.L. Jones took this typical American elk in November 1934, it wasn't until 1948 that it was measured, recording a spread of 51-4/8 inches. Jones was hunting near Granite Meadows in Umatilla County, Oregon, when he took this bull.

1931

While in Cassiar, British Columbia, Canada, on September 6, 1931, Major James Workman harvested this Stone's sheep. After traveling back to his home in Nottinghill Belfast in Northern Ireland, Rowland Ward Ltd. took measurements from the unmounted specimen and recorded a tip-to-tip a spread of 25-4/8 inches.

1952

The current Montana state record Shiras' moose was measured by Samuel B. Webb and Grancel Fitz in 1952 and scores 195-1/8 points. This trophy bull was taken in the Red Rock Lakes Refuge in Beaverhead County by C.M. Schmauch.

On September 18, 1960, Randolph J. Brill took this barren ground caribou, scoring 382-5/8 points. Being from Wisconsin, Brill enlisted the help of a guide named Frenchy Lamoureux to navigate the Talkeena Mountains in Alaska.

1960

Dr. Moore is 6 feet 1*11 himself.

1934

Kentucky doctor Chas. H. Moore made his trip to Kodiak Island's Terror Bay very rewarding when he harvested this Alaska brown bear on May 24, 1934. Along with the length from tip of nose to tip of tail recorded at 8 feet 2 inches, it was also noted that the sagittal and occipital areas of the skull were slightly damaged. (Typed on photo: Moore is 6 feet tall himself.)

Daniel E. Osborne was hunting 40 miles west of Red Bluff in Tehama County, California, on August 14, 1956, when he took this typical Columbia blacktail deer scoring 132-6/8 points.

1960

Walter J. Wojciuk, from Milwaukee Wisconsin, was guided by local Frenchy Lamoureux through the Talkeetna Mountains, Alaska. In September 1960 he took this barren ground caribou. His trophy, which scores 411-7/8 points, was measured and mounted by Jonas Brothers of Denver.

1927

Years after Paul H. Temple took his typical American elk, his son Gary entered it in the Club's 25th Awards Program. With a score of 377-4/8 inches, this great trophy is proof that back in November 1927, Jefferson County, Montana, was producing record bulls. On this occasion, Temple was joined by W.E. Talent and Jack Keenan and used a Savage Model 99 to harvest this records-book bull elk sporting a 53-2/8 inch spread.

1938

Harvard A. Middling took this barren ground caribou on September 20, 1938, while hunting in Rainy Pass, Alaska. It has a spread of 39-4/8 inches.

Nils Danielson, from Sweden, took this Alaska-Yukon moose in 1954.

1954

Heading north from Allentown, Pennsylvania, Phillip Neuweiler relied on guide Walter Carlick to navigate Level Mountains, British Columbia, Canada, where he successfully harvested this mountain caribou. His trophy bull scores 402-4/8 points.

1956

In 1936, Moose Flats on the Kenai Peninsula in Alaska, was deserving of its name after yielding this Alaska-Yukon moose to George B. Petty on a fall hunt with his buddies. This trophy was noted to have the palms folded, no front palm, and a spread of 70-4/8 inches.

1953

On September 1, 1953, Ray Al Winchester went on a solo hunt around Snow Shoe Lake, Alaska, and harvested this barren ground caribou. With a score of 440-7/8 points, it was presented with the 1st Place Award for the 6th Competition. In 1954, the Demarest Memorial Foundation purchased the rack for $150.

Unfortunately all that is known about this trophy is what is written on the front of this postcard. Only the hunter's first name, Larry, is decipherable along with the location this typical American elk was taken, Valley Ranch in Valley, Wyoming.

Record elk—owned by Larry Larom—Valley Ranch Valley—Wyo—

In August 1956, Charles Brumbelow was solo hunting for barren ground caribou near Hicks Creek, Alaska, when he successfully took this bull. U.S. Air Force Captain Lewis E. Yearout, a wildlife conservation officer of the Alaskan Air Command, gave it a score of 418-5/8 points.

1956

1934

In fall of 1934, J.A. Thacker crossed the border into Las Varas, Chihuahua, Mexico, to harvest this pronghorn. Once back home in El Paso, Texas, Thacker put his trophy—with a spread of 14-3/8 inches and a tip to tip of 8-7/8 inches—on display in his wholesale dry goods store, Thacker and Baca.

Philip A. Johnson and John N. Brennan shot simultaneously at this Dall's sheep on August 26, 1950. The ram was taken on the north fork of the Johnson River, approximately 25 miles off the Alaska Highway. With a score of 180-3/8 points, it was awarded 1st Place during the 4th Competition. Philip A. Johnson is pictured here with their trophy.

1950

1947

In 1947, Frank L. Vennum went on two productive hunts. The first was in October to the Sawtooth Blue Mountains, Washington, where he took a typical mule deer. On the second, he harvested a typical American elk, with a 52-4/8-inch spread, from Umatilla County, Oregon. Unfortunately both trophies were destroyed in a fire in 1950.

Guide Bill Hutchison, from Casper, Wyoming, met with Kevin Kearns, from Creve Coeur, Missouri in September 1961. Hutchison took Kearns to Fremont County, Wyoming, where he harvested this pronghorn, scoring 81 points.

1961

1935

In 1935, this grizzly bear was harvested by R.H. Johnson near Ball Creek, a tributary of the Iskoot River, which empties into the Stickine River just above the Alaska boundary. Johnson's .300 Savage dropped this bear with a bullet between the eyes at a distance of 8 feet. The paw measured 8 inches wide and the fat on the rump was 5 inches thick.

Bud W. L. Jump lived in the area of Juniper Mountain, Arizona, when he took this pronghorn (circled) September 25, 1960. The bucks measures 81 points.

1960

1911

The state of Wyoming must have been amazed when Prince Nicolas Ghika from Comanesti Bacau Romania arrived the summer of 1911 to hunt in the Bighorn Mountains. He took this typical American elk. It wasn't until 1931 when Princess Yvonne Ghika submitted the measurements of the late prince's bull. The original measurement, taken in centimeters, had a spread of 83 centimeters or 32-5/8 inches. The measurements were recorded in *Rowland Ward's Records of Big Game*.

Lloyd L. Ward, Jr., traveled from Blytheville, Arkansas, in the fall of 1947 to go on a guided hunt in British Columbia. Guide Jack Lewis led him to Harrison Lake near Vancouver, where he harvested this typical Columbia blacktail. There was a statement that the first points were only buds about 6/8 inch long, and the left antler was broken from fighting, giving it a score of 145-2/8 points.

1947

This fine trophy typical whitetail deer weighed 203 pounds at field dressing and was measured at 164-2/8 points. Leon Richards was bowhunting on Howland Island, New York, in November 1955 when he took this buck.

1955

Local to the area, Rudy C. Grecar was hunting in Geauga County, Ohio, in October 1969, when he took this non-typical whitetail deer. He was bowhunting and hit this buck, scoring 200-4/8 points, from 35 yards.

1969

As a registered guide and outfitter from Chisana, Alaska, Larry Folger knew the area well when he took his grizzly bear in September 1957. Grancel and Betty Fitz measured the bear for Folger, giving it a score of 24-14/16 points.

1957

September 25, 1952, was the day that guide Harold Jameson took Ralph A. Fry up Ram River, Alberta, Canada, where he harvested this typical American elk before returning home to Kansas. The bull had some distinct qualities. "One abnormal point on the right side and the sixth point on the right side might not count, as the base almost equals the length, giving the bull a score of 399-2/8 points."

1952

In 1952, J.J. Hartnett was hunting pronghorn in the Lance Creek area near Manville, Wyoming, when he took this buck scoring 86-2/8 points.

1952

1933

Enlarged from Movie film. Freeman's Caribou

Freeman's Caribou

A.B. Freeman, from New Orleans, Louisiana, was on a hunting trip near Rainy
Pass, Alaska, in 1933 when he harvested this barren ground caribou. It was
measured by Frederic W. Miller at the Colorado Museum of Natural History.
The photo of Freeman in the field (left) was reproduced from movie film.

1953

1935

LEFT: John Treillet planned a hunting trip from Gloversville, New York, to Kodiak Island, Alaska, in September 1953. With his guide, Pinnell Talifson, Treillet took this Alaska brown bear on September 22. His trophy scores 28-11/16 points.

RIGHT: On September 25, 1935, H.S. Compton took this unique pronghorn 20 miles southwest of Cody, Wyoming. It has a spread of 14-5/8 inches and the prongs on right and left sides are somewhat recurved and with two tines. It was also noted that the horns are exceptionally rugose.

John Caputo, Sr., and his guide Buck Sanford posed with this magnificent typical American elk, scoring 380-6/8 points, taken near Park County, Montana, in 1968.

1968

1977

In 1977 Myles T. Keller went bowhunting in Burnett County, Wisconsin, and skillfully harvested this typical whitetail deer scoring 174-7/8 points.

Keith Chisholm took this Alaska brown bear near Frazer Lake on Kodiak Island, Alaska, in 1956. Assuming he traveled with family from Las Cruces, New Mexico, at the young age of 11, this bear was quite a trophy, scoring 29-7/16 points.

1956

A BIG MTN.
SHEEP
RIGGA

1906

While hunting near Yarrow Creek in Alberta F.H. Riggall took this bighorn sheep on December 14, 1906. It has a "massive" mid-section and when it was measured in 1952, after 45 years, the skull and horns still weighed 31 pounds and scored 193-6/8 points. A letter sent from Riggall in 1952 stated, "Mr. Jack O'Connor of *Outdoor Life* saw it last year and said it was the largest head he had ever personally examined. He spent an hour with it!"

Even though this trophy was not taken in North America, the score chart and details made its way to the Boone and Crockett Club. Philip Maurice was hunting near the Glaisnock River in Te-Anau, New Zealand, when he took this red deer in 1952. It was measured at 397-6/8 points, but the notes indicated a possible variance with a 2-inch point growing on first point of the right antler. Also, the "crown points" beyond the royal are typical of red deer. Some would be considered abnormal on a wapiti, which would reduce the score.

1946

Dick Gaudern was on a solo hunt September, 1946 when he took this Shiras' moose. The bull was taken near Ditch Creek in Teton County, Wyoming, received a First Award for the 7th Competition and is still ranked 14th in the state. The picture to the far left of the mount on the back of Gaudern's Dodge sedan was to show scale.

On November 1, 1962 Del Austin took this non-typical whitetail deer, scoring 277-3/8 points, in Hall County, Nebraska. He received Second Award for the 11th Competition. This buck is still ranks second in the state.

NON-TYPICAL WHITETAIL

1961

Kenny McRae's record cougar tipped the scale at 172 pounds and scored 15-3/16 points. He took his trophy November 5, 1961, near Trout Creek in Alberta.

At the young age of 16 years, Stanley B. Fredenburgh, Jr. traveled from New York to Quebec. He was hunting near Turcotte Lake when he harvested this Canada moose. With three abnormal points on back of right palm it scored 202-2/8 points.

1962

Donald R. Vaughn took this typical whitetail deer while hunting in Henderson County, Illinois, October 29, 1960. This buck had one abnormal point extending forward from burr on right antler and weighed 306 pounds. It scored 170 points.

1960

George F. Stewart, Jr., was on a solo hunt in Glenn County, California, in October 1957 when he harvested this typical Columbia blacktail. It was measured by the patrol captain of California Department of Fish and Game and scores 149-4/8 points.

1957

Travelling from Ohio to Alaska, Dr. Russell J. Uhl was successful in harvesting this Alaska brown bear April 25, 1963. He was hunting near Fog Creek on the Alaska Peninsula when he took his trophy. With a score of 29-12/16 points, it received the 2nd Award for the 11th competition and is now owned by Cabela's.

ACKNOWLEDGEMENTS
VINTAGE HUNTING ALBUM

Vice President of Communications
Marc C. Mondavi

Publications Committee Chair
Howard P. Monsour, Jr.

Publications Committee Deputy Chair
Kyle C. Krause

Director of Publications
Julie T. Houk

Introduction written by:
Kyle C. Krause
Boone and Crockett Club Regular Member
Fair Chase Magazine Hunting and Ethics Editor

Images researched and selected from the Boone and Crockett Club's Archives in Missoula, Montana by:
Julie T. Houk
Wendy Nickelson
Karlie Slayer

Copy Edited by:
Julie Cowan
Missoula, Montana

Vintage Hunting Album was designed by Karlie Slayer, Designer, with the assistance of Julie T. Houk, Director of Publication, for the Boone and Crockett Club using American Typewriter® typeface.

American Typewriter is a style of typeface created in 1974 by Joel Kaden and Tony Stan for International Typeface Corporation based on the form and monospaced feature of the early Sholes's patent of the typewriter. The typewriter was patented in 1868 by Christopher Latham Sholes, who sold his rights to the Remington Arms Company in 1873. The first typewriters were initially thought to be replacements for printing and so typewriter keybars utilized printing types; monospaced typefaces, that is, those designed so every letter takes up the same amount of space were a more practical alternative and soon replaced printing types.

Printed and Bound in Canada by:
Friesens